GEOGRAPHY NOW!

MOUNTAINS

AROUND THE WORLD

JEN GREEN

PowerKiDS press
New York

Published in 2009 by The Rosen Publishing Group Inc.
29 East 21st Street, New York, NY 10010

First Edition

Editor: Jon Richards
Designer: Ben Ruocco
Consultant: John Williams

Library of Congress Cataloging-in-Publication Data

Green, Jen.
Mountains around the world / Jen Green. – 1st ed.
p. cm. – (Geography now)
Includes index.
ISBN 978-1-4358-2869-8 (library binding)
ISBN 978-1-4358-2955-8 (paperback)
ISBN 978-1-4358-2961-9 (6-pack)
1. Mountains–Juvenile literature. I. Title.
GB512.G76 2009
551.43'2–dc22

2008025762

Manufactured in China

Picture acknowledgments:
(t-top, b-bottom, l-left, r-right, c-center)
Front cover Dreamstime.com/Jose Fuente, 1 Dreamstime.com/Mcech, 4-5 Dreamstime.com/Scott Miller, 4bl Dreamstime.com/Lambert Parren, 5br istockphoto.com/Vladimir Melnik, 6-7 Dreamstime.com/Paul Prescott, 7tr istockphoto.com/Jurga Rubinovaite, 7br istockphoto.com/John Heaton, 8-9 istockphoto.com/Steve Elsworth, 8bl istockphoto.com/ Colin Soutar, 9br istockphoto.com/Bruce Bean, 10-11 Dreamstime.com, 10cl Dreamstime.com/Rick Parsons, 11br istockphoto.com/Bruce Bean, 12-13 istockphoto.com/Robert Frith, 12bl Dreamstime.com/Bayon, 13br Ear1grey/GNU Free documentation license, 14-15 Dreamstime.com/Juan Lobo, 14bl Dreamstime.com/ Mike Norton, 15br Dreamstime.com/Grigory Kubatyan, 16-17 Dreamstime.com/Dmitry Pichugin, 16bl Dreamstime.com/Peter Hazlett, 17br Dreamstime.com/Jörg Jahn, 18-19 Dreamstime.com/ Ferdericb, 18bl istockphoto.com/Saso Novoselic, 19br Dreamstime.com/Marcin Czarnoleski, 20-21 Dreamstime.com/Piccaya, 20bl istockphoto.com, 21br Dreamstime.com/Pavalache Stelian, 22-23 Dreamstime.com/Mcech, 22bl and 23br Dreamstime.com/Xdrew, 24-25 Dreamstime.com/Cora Reed, 24bl Underwood & Underwood/Corbis, 25br Dreamstime.com/Galina Barskaya, 26-27 istockphoto.com/ Stephan Hoerold, 26bl istockphoto.com/William Walsh, 27br istockphoto.com/Daniel Stein, 28-29 Dreamstime.com/Simon Gurney, 28cb Dreamstime.com/Tan Wei Ming, 29br Dreamstime.com/Tamas

CONTENTS

What are mountains?

Mountains are large masses of rock that rise above the surrounding landscape. High ground above 3,280 ft. (1,000 m) is generally considered to be a mountain, but definitions of mountains vary. What is thought to be a high mountain in Britain would be a mere hill among the world's highest peaks.

Every continent on Earth has craggy mountains. These are the Grand Teton Range in Wyoming. Mountain chains are also found rising from the ocean floor.

Most mountains occur in groups called ranges. Peaks that stand alone are usually volcanoes. This volcano, Mount Fuji, is Japan's highest mountain.

HARSH CONDITIONS

High mountains have a cold, snowy climate. This is because air becomes thinner as you get higher, and "thin" air holds less of the sun's heat. Snow falls in cold temperatures and builds up on mountain summits. Thin air also contains less oxygen, which is why mountaineers often breathe bottled air.

HABITATS AND RESOURCES

Mountain plants and animals are suited to the cold climate. The people who live on mountain slopes make use of resources such as farmland and minerals. The rugged scenery also attracts tourists, but such human activity can lead to pollution and other problems.

Sacred peaks

Towering, snow-capped mountains are an awe-inspiring sight. In ancient times, people believed that gods lived on some mountains, such as Mount Olympus in Greece and Mount Kailash in Tibet. Pilgrims still visit remote mountains to pay their respects to the gods. Some peaks are considered too sacred to be climbed.

A pilgrim gazes at the snowy peaks of the Himalayas. Local people believe that some Himalayan peaks are sacred.

How do mountains form?

Mountains form when rocks near the Earth's surface are pushed upward. This upheaval is caused by the movement of giant slabs of thick rock, called tectonic plates, that make up the Earth's crust. There are three types of mountains: fold mountains, block mountains, and volcanoes.

Young fold mountains, such as the Himalayas, are still being pushed upward. These mountains are growing several inches taller every year.

FOLD MOUNTAINS

The Earth's tectonic plates ride like rafts on the red-hot, molten rock below the crust. Driven by swirling currents in the layer below, the plates drift very slowly over the surface, colliding, scraping past one another, or pulling apart. Where tectonic plates collide, the crust between them crumples upward to form a range of fold mountains. The Himalayas formed when the tectonic plate bearing India crashed into Asia about 50 million years ago.

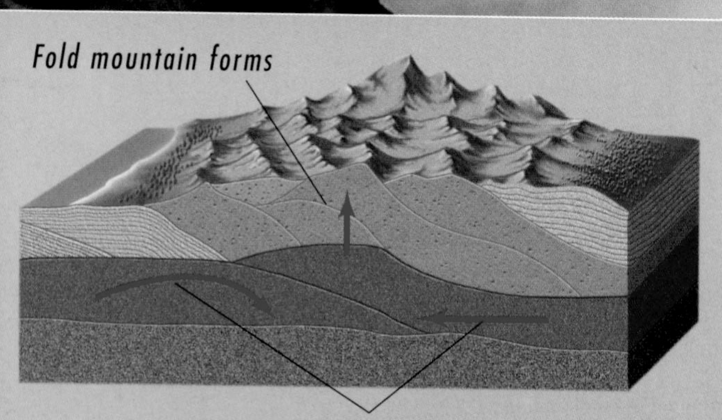

Fold mountains rise as the crusts of two tectonic plates crash together and are crumpled into folds.

BLOCK MOUNTAINS

Block mountains start to form when the movement of tectonic plates causes rocks to shatter. Deep cracks called faults appear in surface rocks. Where a giant slab of rock is forced upward between two faults by pressures in the Earth's crust, a block mountain forms. When slabs of rock pull apart at a fault, they can collapse to form a rift valley. Erosion of softer rock can leave behind sheer cliffs.

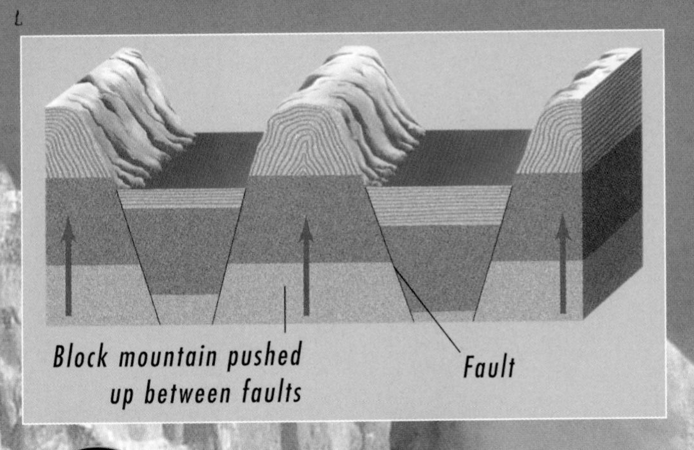

This diagram (left) shows how block mountains form as rocks are forced upward between faults. Mount Rundle in Canada (above) is a block mountain.

Volcanoes

Volcanoes form where molten rock, called magma, wells up from below the Earth's crust and bursts through a weak point. Lava spills out onto the surface, hardens, and builds up to form a cone-shaped mountain. Most volcanoes erupt along plate boundaries, where two tectonic plates are pulling apart.

Volcanic mountains are made of hardened lava, ash, and cinders. This is Mount Rainier in Washington state.

Wearing away

Mountains may look solid and unchanging, but even these enormous masses of rock do not last forever. Slowly but steadily, they are worn away by wind, water, frost, and ice, in a process called erosion. Over millions of years, high, craggy mountains wear away to become low, rounded hills.

These mountains in the Scottish Highlands were once high and jagged. Millions of years of erosion have worn them into lower, rugged slopes.

Where glaciers flow down a mountain on all sides, they can carve a steep-sided peak called a horn. The Matterhorn in Switzerland (below) is an example of this.

WATER AND ICE EROSION

Water and ice are the main forces of erosion in mountain regions. Streams and rivers loosen and carry away rock, gradually carving narrow, V-shaped valleys. Water seeping into rocky crevices freezes at night and expands to split the rocks. Where snow builds up on a high peak, it forms a glacier. These "rivers of ice" slowly bulldoze their way downhill, carving deep, U-shaped valleys.

MASS WASTING

Erosion is usually slow, but sometimes a mass of rock breaks away at once in a landslide. As this roars downhill, it dislodges more debris and picks up speed. When a mass of snow and rock slides away, it is called an avalanche. The rapid erosion caused by landslides and avalanches is called mass wasting. It is often triggered by heavy rain or snow.

Volcanic plugs

Volcanic eruptions often end when a mass of magma plugs the crater of a volcano. The magma cools to form a column of very hard rock. Over many years, the softer layers of ash and lava that covered the plug are worn away to leave a tall, rocky pillar.

Devil's Tower, Wyoming, is an example of a volcanic plug.

Climate and wildlife

Mountains have a harsher climate than lowland regions, with snow, ice, and whistling winds. The temperature drops 2°F (1°C) for every 500 feet (150 meters) you climb. Windy conditions bring rapidly changing weather, with mist, sunshine, rain, hail, and thunderstorms, often in a single day.

Chamois live high in the Alps in Europe. A dense, hairy coat helps these goats to survive in freezing conditions. Rubbery hooves allow them to climb sheer rock.

MOUNTAIN ANIMALS

Animals that live on mountains are equipped for the harsh conditions there. Goats and llamas have thick fur, and mountain birds have dense feathers. Some animals visit the upper pastures in the summer and retreat down the mountain in the winter. Snakes and marmots spend the winter in their dens, in a deep sleep called hibernation.

VEGETATION ZONES

Mountain plants have to be tough to cope with cold, frosty conditions and a short growing season. They grow in thin and stony soil. As the air gets colder at greater heights, a series of vegetation zones develops. Lower slopes may be covered with forests, but only low-growing shrubs and grasses thrive beyond a point called the treeline. Summits often have no plants—just bare rock and snow.

This photograph of the Rocky Mountains shows the treeline in the foreground. Here, the trees thin out and low-growing grasses take over. The summits in the background are bare rock covered with snow.

Rain shadows

Mountain slopes facing the ocean are always the wettest part of mountains. As winds blow inland, the damp air rises and cools. The moisture condenses (cools and collects) to produce rain-bearing clouds. The far side of the mountain, called the rain shadow, is shielded from the wet winds and receives very little rain.

Ladakh in southern Asia is very dry, because the immense bulk of the Himalayas shields it from wet winds.

Using mountains

Mountainous areas are often used for farming. Valuable minerals may be found there, forests provide timber and fuel, and streams can be used to produce energy. About 10 percent of the world's population lives in the high valleys between mountain summits.

Lhasa in Tibet is one of the highest cities in the world. Tourists come to visit the Potala Palace, former home of Tibet's spiritual leader, the Dalai Lama.

MINING AND TOURISM

Gold, silver, copper, uranium, and even diamonds are mined in some mountains. Pure white marble for sculptures is quarried at Carrara, in the Apennine Mountains in Italy. Since the mid-1900s, the tourism industry has grown rapidly. People come to mountainous areas to ski in the winter, or to hike, climb, or enjoy newer sports, such as hang gliding and mountain biking, in the summer.

FARMING

Farming in mountain regions is not easy. The thin soil and harsh climate produce difficult growing conditions. On steep slopes, farmers often dig terraces to create flat land for farming. Animals such as goats, sheep, and cattle can be pastured on land that is too steep or stony for crops. Herders lead their animals up the mountain for the summer and down again for the winter.

Cows graze a high pasture in the Alps. In the winter, these slopes will be covered with snow, and the cows will shelter in lowland barns.

Hydroelectric power

The gushing water of mountain streams can be harnessed to produce hydroelectricity. A dam is built above the power station to ensure an even flow of water. The water rushes through turbines, which work generators to produce electricity. Reservoirs created by the dams supply lowland towns with water.

These turbines, inside one of seven hydroelectric plants in Australia's Snowy Mountains, help to supply 10 percent of the electricity needs of New South Wales.

Protecting mountains

Activities such as farming, forestry, mining, and tourism can harm wild mountain areas, causing erosion and pollution. Scientists are looking for ways to use mountain resources without damaging the environment. This is called sustainable development.

FARMING AND LOGGING

Forestry and farming can cause erosion on steep slopes. The roots of trees and plants form an underground network that holds the soil in place. When the natural vegetation is stripped off, the soil can wash away quickly, and landslides become more common. Selective logging and building terraces can help to preserve the soil.

Landslides are common on slopes that have been stripped of all timber. Selective logging—cutting clumps of trees here and there—does less harm.

The ground around this copper mine in the Andes has been stripped of vegetation to allow copper to be extracted. Heaps of waste rock are left around the mine, polluting the environment.

TOURISTS AND MINING

Mining produces widespread erosion, and also pollutes mountain air, soil, and streams. Even tourists can cause erosion, because boots and skis strip away the soil and trample fragile plants. When remote mountains are opened up for tourism or mining, new roads, railroads, and airports are built. These activities change the natural environment. One way to preserve untouched areas is to set aside land for national parks.

Protecting rare animals

Mountain animals are often threatened by human activity. Logging and mining deprive animals of their homes, and hunting has rapidly reduced the numbers of some types of deer and birds. Conservation can help save rare species, such as condors. Birds are bred in captivity and then released into the wild.

An Andean condor soars high above a mountain, scanning for dead animals. With a wingspan of 10 ft. (3 m), it is one of the world's biggest birds.

Earth's highest mountain

Mount Everest

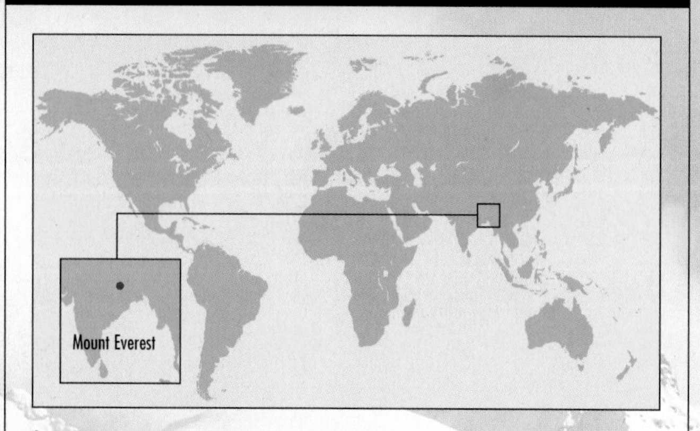

STATISTICS

- Location: Himalayas, southern Central Asia
- Type of mountain: Fold mountain
- Height: 29,035 ft. (8,850 m)
- Largest nearby town: Namche Bazaar
- Main industries: Farming, tourism (including mountaineering)
- Environmental issues: Deforestation, erosion, litter

The world's tallest mountain, Mount Everest, lies between Nepal and Tibet. Everest is part of the Himalayan range that stretches across northern India. In the west, the Himalayas merge with the Karakorum mountain range. The ten highest peaks on Earth are all found in these two ranges.

Modern climbing expeditions need huge amounts of food and equipment. This is mostly carried up the mountain by Sherpas.

Mount Everest is named after Sir George Everest, who led the survey team in the 1800s that recognized the world's highest peak. The local name, Chomolungma, means "Goddess mother of the world."

LOCAL PEOPLE AND CLIMBERS

The foothills of Everest have been settled for centuries by people such as the Sherpa, who grow crops and keep shaggy beasts called yaks for their milk and meat, and as pack animals. Everest was first climbed in 1953 by a Sherpa climber, Tenzing Norgay, and a New Zealander, Edmund Hillary.

TOURISM AND CONSERVATION

Tourism is now a leading industry around Mount Everest. Foreign visitors leave litter ranging from candy wrappers to oxygen cylinders on the mountain. Local forests are felled to build lodges for tourists, causing landslides. Fortunately, Everest is now a protected area. Tourists pay park fees, which help to fund conservation work.

Sherpa capital

Namche Bazaar is the largest settlement near Everest. This market town has expanded rapidly because of tourism, especially following the construction of an airstrip at Lukla, a day's walk away. Climbers and trekkers pass through Namche on their way to Everest Base Camp.

Namche Bazaar lies on a high shoulder of rock below the summit of Mount Everest.

Africa's highest peak

Mount Kilimanjaro

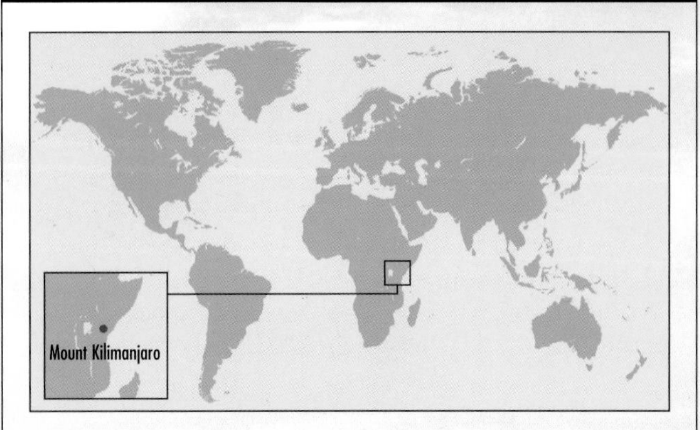

STATISTICS

- *Location: Tanzania, East Africa*
- *Type of mountain: Volcanic*
- *Height: 19,340 ft. (5,895 m)*
- *Largest nearby town: Moshi, Tanzania*
- *Main industries: Farming, some tourism*
- *Environmental issues: Summit snow is melting*

The snow-capped dome of Mount Kilimanjaro rises from the plains of East Africa. Africa's tallest summit is also the world's highest free-standing mountain—one that is not part of any range. Like most other isolated peaks, it is a volcano—or rather, three volcanoes that erupted virtually on top of one another, but are no longer active.

Trekkers pass through the bleak landscape of the alpine zone on their way to the summit of Kilimanjaro.

VEGETATION ZONES

The vegetation zones found at different heights on mountains are clearly defined on Kilimanjaro. Tropical rain forests cover the foothills. Beyond the treeline is a bleak heath and moorland zone, and above that, an alpine zone of grassy pasture. The summit is bare and snow-covered. Botanists compare the vegetation seen while climbing Kilimanjaro to that encountered on a huge journey all the way from the equator to the poles.

The towering peak of Kilimanjaro is an amazing sight—a snow-capped mountain only 186 miles (300 km) from the equator.

CLIMBING KILIMANJARO

The main industries in the foothills of Kilimanjaro are farming and tourism. This mountain can be scaled in less than a week, but climbers can get altitude sickness because of the thin air at great heights. The first symptoms are feeling sick and dizzy, but the condition can be fatal. The only cure is to descend.

Giant plants

Most plants that grow high on mountains grow close to the ground, to avoid howling winds. Two tall plants in Kilimanjaro's moorland zone are an exception. The giant lobelia produces a tall spike of flowers up to 10 ft. (3 m) high. The giant groundsel is even more impressive, growing to 16 ft. (5 m).

The giant lobelia has a crown of large leaves topped by a tall spike covered in tiny blue flowers.

Earth's longest range

The Andes

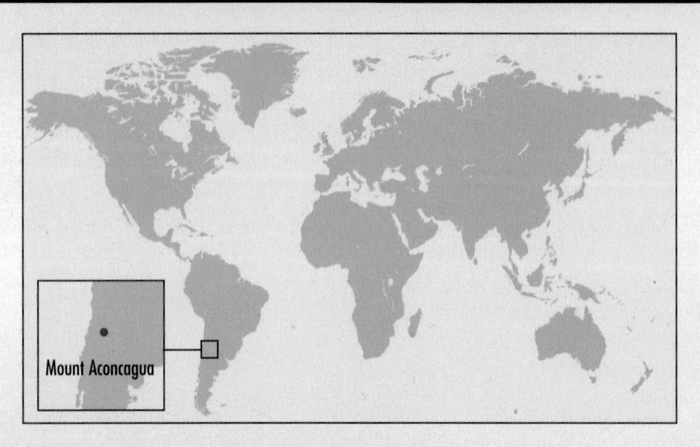

STATISTICS

- *Location: Western South America*
- *Type of mountain: Fold mountains, some volcanic peaks*
- *Highest peak: Aconcagua, Argentina: 22,835 ft. (6,960 m)*
- *Largest cities: La Paz, Bogotá, Cuzco, Quito*
- *Main industries: Mining, farming, some tourism*
- *Environmental issues: Pollution from industry, erosion*

At 12,500 ft. (3,811 m), Lake Titicaca is the world's highest navigable lake. The local people, the Aymara, sail the lake in boats made of reeds.

The Andes are the world's longest mountain chain, about 4,500 miles (7,200 km) long. The range runs virtually the whole length of South America, from Venezuela to the southern tip of Chile. Landscapes include snowy peaks, grassy plains called paramos, and shimmering lakes.

FORMATION

The Andes were formed by the Earth's crust folding and also by volcanic activity. The source of this upheaval lies offshore, on the ocean bed. Here, two of the Earth's tectonic plates collide, and one is forced below the other. Deep below ground, the crust melts and then rises upward to form a line of volcanic peaks in the Andes.

EMPIRES AND MINERALS

In ancient times, the lower slopes of the Andes were settled by various people, including the Incas. Between the 1100s and 1500s CE, the Incas ruled over a mountain empire from their Andean capital, Cuzco. In the 1500s, the Incas were conquered by the Spanish, who came in search of gold and silver. The region is still known for its mineral riches, and mining settlements, such as Potosí in Bolivia, have become major cities.

The snowy peaks of the world's highest volcanoes are found in the Andes. Since prehistoric times, people have terraced the lower slopes of these mountains to grow potatoes and corn.

Machu Picchu

The Incas were skilled builders. Their magnificent stonework can still be seen in Cuzco and at the mountain retreat of Machu Picchu. This city became a refuge for the Incas during the Spanish conquest, but was finally abandoned. It was rediscovered by the U.S. archaeologist, Hiram Bingham, in 1911.

The ruins of Machu Picchu stand on a ledge high above the River Urubamba, overshadowed by a lofty peak.

Europe's well-loved peaks

The Alps

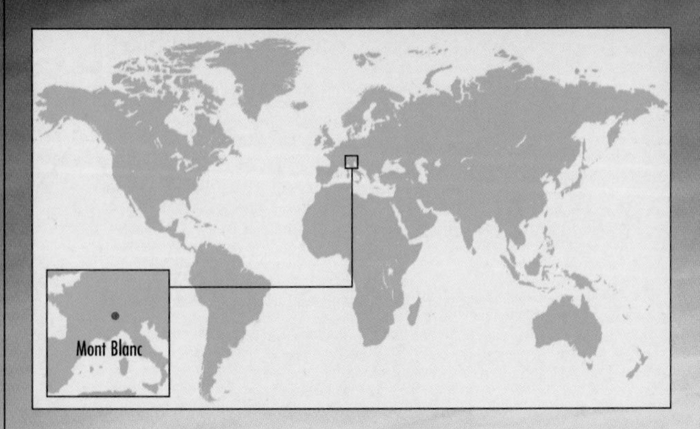

STATISTICS

- *Location: Southern central Europe*
- *Type of mountain: Fold mountains*
- *Highest peak: Mont Blanc, France: 15,785 ft. (4,810 m)*
- *Largest towns: Chamonix, Lucerne, Cortina, Salzburg*
- *Main industries: Tourism, farming, manufacturing*
- *Environmental issues: Pollution, pressure from tourism*

The Alps are Europe's highest mountains, stretching eastward from France across northern Italy, Switzerland, and Austria as far as Hungary. This range is 621 miles (1,000 km) long and was formed by folding. Tourism and transportation are well developed in the region, but have led to problems such as air pollution and overcrowding.

Skiing is the main tourist activity in the Alps in the winter. Resorts such as Val Thorens, France, have been built for skiing, at the foot of high, snowy slopes.

ALPINE INDUSTRIES

The original inhabitants of the Alps were the Celts. They raised crops and livestock, and mined minerals in high valleys from around 800 BCE. Farmers led sheep and cattle to high pastures for the summer and brought them down for the winter. Tourism began about 200 years ago, when people began to visit Alpine spas—towns whose waters were believed to cure sickness.

The high, jagged peaks of the Alps were carved by glaciers.

THE RISE OF TOURISM

Over 12 million tourists now visit the Alps each year. Downhill skiing has been popular since the 1930s. From the late 1800s, the construction of roads, railroads, and later airports opened up the Alps for trade and tourism. Trucks and cars laboring up mountain roads pollute the clear air, however, so a few resorts, such as Wengen in Switzerland, are now car-free zones.

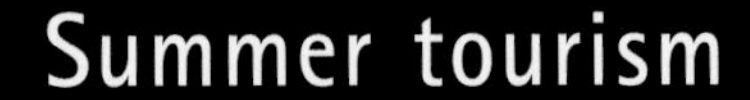

Summer tourism

Tourism in the Alps is not restricted to the winter months. In the summer, millions of vacationers travel to the Alps to enjoy the scenery. The steep slopes that were used for skiing are now used for hiking and mountain biking.

Some visitors prefer pedal power to other forms of transportation. Others are content to let chairlifts and cable cars carry them to the peaks.

Mountain towns

The Rockies

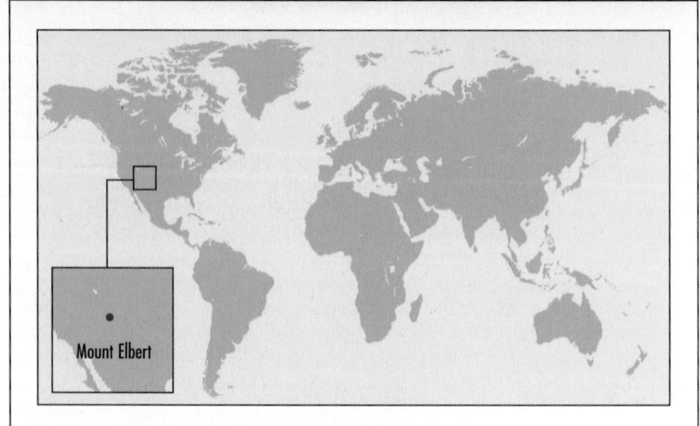

STATISTICS

- *Location: Western North America*
- *Type of mountain: Fold mountains*
- *Highest peak: Mt. Elbert, Colorado: 14,430 ft. (4,399 m)*
- *Largest cities: Denver, Colorado; Calgary, Canada*
- *Main industries: Farming, mining, manufacturing*
- *Environmental issues: Pollution from mining and industry*

The Rocky Mountains form the world's second-longest mountain chain, running for 2,980 miles (4,800 km) down the western side of North America. This towering range forms what is called the Continental Divide, separating rivers flowing west to the Pacific Ocean and east to the Atlantic.

This archive photograph from the 1800s shows a prospector crouching over a river, panning for gold.

MINERAL RICHES

The chief industries of the Rockies include livestock farming, logging, and mining. The mountains are a source of gold, silver, copper, lead, zinc, and coal. In 1859, the discovery of gold in the Colorado Rockies brought many to the region. The range formed a great barrier for pioneers wanting to settle in the Far West. Wagon trains crossed the divide via a high pass on the Overland Trail.

GROWTH OF A MOUNTAIN TOWN

Denver, Colorado, is one of the largest settlements in the Rockies. It was founded as a mining town during the gold rush of the 1860s, but unlike many mining settlements, it did not become a deserted "ghost town" when the minerals ran out. Denver developed into a center for ranching and a stop on stagecoach and railroad routes. It is now a thriving business center, with over 550,000 inhabitants.

Denver is known as the Mile High City, because it is at such a high altitude. Some of the peaks of the Rockies can be seen in the distance.

Parks and resorts

The Rockies are now a major center for tourism. Many visitors pass through Denver on their way to the Rocky Mountain National Park. The nearby towns of Aspen and Vail are modern ski resorts. The region's parks include Yellowstone in Wyoming. Founded in 1872, Yellowstone was the world's first national park.

Snowboarding is popular in ski resorts such as Vail and Aspen.

Preserving the wilderness

Yosemite National Park

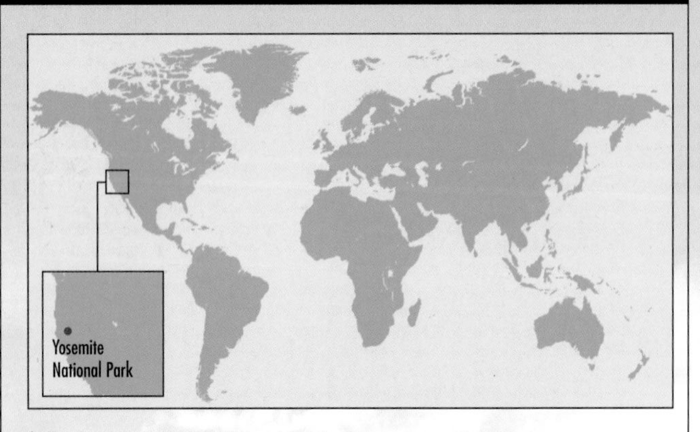

STATISTICS

- *Location: Sierra Nevada Mountains, California*
- *Type of mountain: Fold mountains, some volcanic peaks*
- *Highest point: Mount Whitney: 14,505 ft. (4,421 m)*
- *Nearest town: Oakhurst*
- *Main industries: Tourism*
- *Environmental issues: Air pollution from vehicles, litter*

Yosemite is a wilderness area covering 1,190 sq miles (3,080 sq km) of the Sierra Nevada Mountains in the western United States. This beautiful region has been a national park since 1890. Park authorities work hard to ensure that the huge numbers of tourists do not harm the very environment they come to see.

Hikers need to obtain a permit to trek the park's 689 miles (1,110 km) of long-distance trails. In the valley, walkers keep to paths to avoid erosion.

Yosemite is known for its rugged scenery, including craggy peaks, sheer rock faces, and glittering lakes. Many of these features were shaped by glaciers.

SHAPED BY ICE

Yosemite Valley is the park's best-known feature. It is a deep, flat-bottomed valley that was carved by a glacier about a million years ago. Small glaciers joining the main valley were cut off by the huge mass of ice flowing below, to form "hanging valleys" ending high on the valley walls. Streams tumble over these sheer cliffs to the floor below.

TOURIST MANAGEMENT

Over 3.5 million tourists visit Yosemite each year. Most of these stay within the valley itself, which represents just 1 percent of the park's total area. Here visitors are encouraged to view the sights using the free bus service rather than private cars, which cause air pollution. Most of the remaining park is true wilderness, where tourism is carefully controlled.

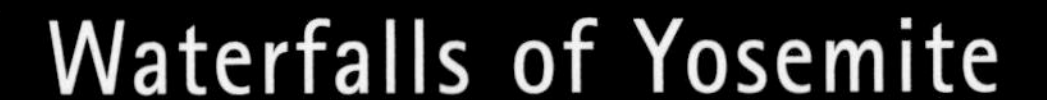

Waterfalls of Yosemite

Yosemite is known for its beautiful waterfalls, which cascade down from hanging valleys. Among the most spectacular is Bridalveil Falls, and Yosemite Falls is the highest waterfall in North America. The falls are at their best when they are fed by melting snow in the springtime.

The water plummets 2,425 ft. (739 m) at Yosemite Falls.

Malaysia's highest peak

Mount Kinabalu

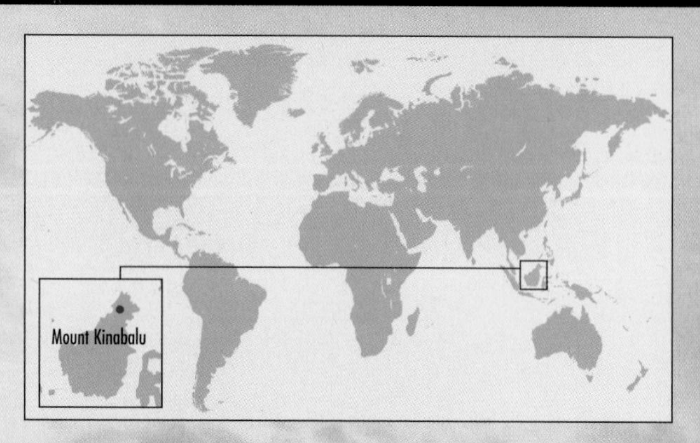

STATISTICS

- *Location: Sabah, Borneo*
- *Type of mountain: Volcanic dome (batholith)*
- *Height: 13,435 ft. (4,095 m)*
- *Nearest town: Kota Kinabalu*
- *Main industries: Tourism in national park*
- *Environmental issues: Collectors threaten some species*

One of the highest mountains in Southeast Asia, Kinabalu lies in the Malaysian part of the island of Borneo. The mountain is in a reserve that covers 290 sq miles (750 sq km). This national park has become a World Heritage site due to its wealth of plants.

Kinabalu is relatively easy to climb and allows hikers to view the mountain's vegetation zones easily. Visitors must obtain a trekking permit and hire a guide before starting the climb.

FORMATION

Kinabalu was formed by magma but is not a volcano. Instead, it is a huge dome of rock called a batholith. Kinabalu began to form when a mass of molten granite rose upward, pushing the rocks above into a dome shape, but cooled before reaching the surface. The softer rocks wore away to expose the granite, which was then carved by glaciers during the last Ice Age.

PLANT LIFE AND CONSERVATION

Kinabalu's tropical climate and high rainfall produce four main vegetation zones at different heights on the peak. The region has about 5,500 plant species—more than Europe and North America combined. The national park has prevented logging, but rare plants are still taken illegally for sale abroad.

Forests at the base of Kinabalu give way to grassy meadows and finally, bare rock near the summit. Glaciers have scoured deep crevices in the rock.

Kinabalu's unique plants

Kinabalu's plant life includes 800 different types of orchids and 600 ferns, with many species that are found nowhere else. Rafflesia plants produce the world's biggest flowers, a yard or more across. There are also highly unusual pitcher plants, which trap and digest insects in their vaselike "pitchers."

Insects slide down into these slippery pitcher plants and are consumed by a pool of digestive juices at the base.

Glossary, Further Information, and Web Sites

ALPINE ZONE
An area of grass and low-growing plants on the upper slopes of a mountain.

ALTITUDE SICKNESS
Symptoms such as dizziness, headache, and nausea, caused by the lack of oxygen in mountain air.

AVALANCHE
A falling mass of snow and rock.

BATHOLITH
A dome of rock that cooled before reaching the Earth's surface and was later exposed by erosion.

BLOCK MOUNTAIN
A type of mountain that forms when a block of rock is forced upward between cracks called faults.

CONDENSE
When water changes from a gas into a liquid.

CONSERVATION
Work done to protect wildlife and places.

CRUST
The Earth's outer layer.

EROSION
When rock or soil is worn away by wind, ice, or water.

FAULT
A deep crack in the rocks of the Earth's crust. Faultlines are often found near the edges of tectonic plates.

FOLD MOUNTAIN
A type of mountain that forms where land crumples upward between colliding tectonic plates.

HORN
A jagged peak carved by glaciers flowing down on all sides.

HYDROELECTRICITY
Electricity generated through the use of fast-flowing water.

ICE AGE
A long, cold period in the Earth's history, during which ice covered more of the land than it does today.

LANDSLIDE
When a mass of rock and soil slips down a mountain.

LAVA
Hot, molten rock from underground that surges to the Earth's surface when a volcano erupts.

MASS WASTING
When a mass of rock, earth, or snow slides downhill in a landslide or avalanche.

NAVIGABLE
A lake or river that boats can sail on.

RAIN SHADOW
A dry area that is shielded from moist winds by a mountain.

SELECTIVE LOGGING
When a few trees are felled without cutting down a whole section of forest.

SUSTAINABLE DEVELOPMENT
A way of using resources that can continue without environmental damage.

TECTONIC PLATES
The giant rocky slabs that make up the Earth's crust.

TREELINE
The zone on a mountain above which trees cannot grow.

TURBINE
A machine powered by water, steam, or gas that is used to generate electricity.

VOLCANIC PLUG
A column of hard volcanic rock that blocks the crater of a volcano and is later exposed by erosion.

VOLCANO
A hole in Earth's crust through which lava and gases pour.

FURTHER READING

Geography Fact Files: Mountains
by Anna Claybourne
(Smart Apple Media, 2004)

The World's Top Ten: Mountain Ranges
by Neil Morris
(Raintree Steck-Vaughn, 1997)

WEB SITES

Due to the changing nature of Internet links, PowerKids Press has developed an online list of Web sites related to the subject of this book. This site is updated regularly. Please use this link to access this list:
www.powerkidslinks.com/geon/mounta

Mountains topic web

Use this topic web to discover themes and ideas in subjects that are related to mountains.

MOUNTAINS

GEOGRAPHY
- How mountains are shaped by water and ice through erosion and mass wasting.
- Natural resources of mountains, such as farmland, minerals, and energy.
- Difficulties of transportation and communication in mountainous areas.

SCIENCE AND THE ENVIRONMENT
- Climate change and Ice Ages, and how they affect mountains.
- Environmental problems, such as pollution, litter, and overdevelopment.
- Conservation work to tackle environmental problems on mountains.

ART AND CULTURE
- Myths and legends about mountains and volcanoes.
- Art, music, and culture of mountain peoples, such as the Sherpa of Nepal.

ENGLISH AND LITERACY
- Accounts of the lives of mountain peoples, such as farmers and miners.
- Debate the pros and cons of development of mountain regions—for example, the building of new resorts.

HISTORY AND ECONOMICS
- History of the use of mountain resources, including faming.
- The development of mountain resorts, towns, and industries.
- Growth of trade and transportation routes in mountain regions.
- History of mountaineering.

Index